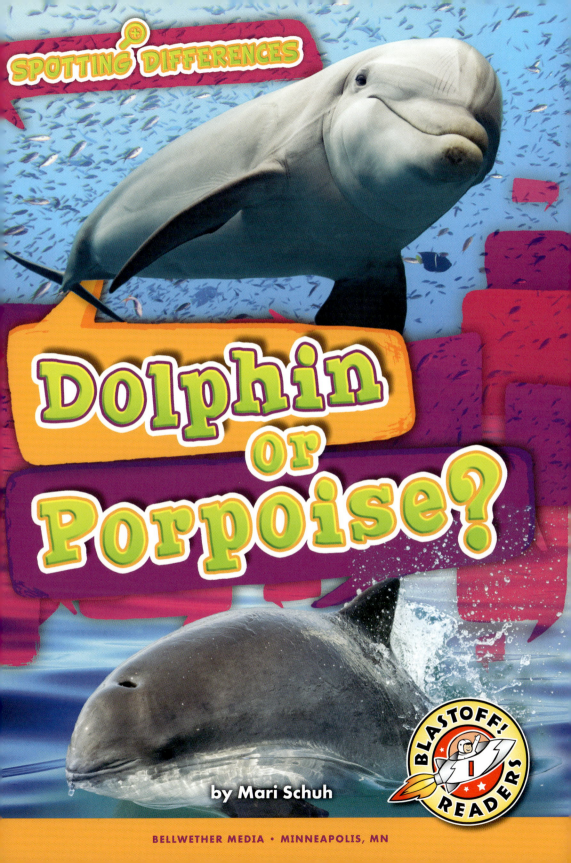

Blastoff! Readers are carefully developed by literacy experts to build reading stamina and move students toward fluency by combining standards-based content with developmentally appropriate text.

 Level 1 provides the most support through repetition of high-frequency words, light text, predictable sentence patterns, and strong visual support.

 Level 2 offers early readers a bit more challenge through varied sentences, increased text load, and text-supportive special features.

 Level 3 advances early-fluent readers toward fluency through increased text load, less reliance on photos, advancing concepts, longer sentences, and more complex special features.

★ **Blastoff! Universe**

Reading Level

 Grade K  Grades 1–3  Grade 4

This edition first published in 2023 by Bellwether Media, Inc.

No part of this publication may be reproduced in whole or in part without written permission of the publisher. For information regarding permission, write to Bellwether Media, Inc., Attention: Permissions Department, 6012 Blue Circle Drive, Minnetonka, MN 55343.

Library of Congress Cataloging-in-Publication Data

Names: Schuh, Mari C., 1975- author.
Title: Dolphin or porpoise? / by Mari Schuh.
Description: Minneapolis, MN : Bellwether Media, Inc., 2023. | Series: Blastoff! readers: spotting differences | Includes bibliographical references and index. | Audience: Ages 5-8 | Audience: Grades K-1 | Summary: "Developed by literacy experts for students in kindergarten through grade three, this book introduces dolphins and porpoises to young readers through leveled text and related photos"-- Provided by publisher.
Identifiers: LCCN 2021062909 (print) | LCCN 2021062910 (ebook) | ISBN 9781644876978 (library binding) | ISBN 9781648347436 (ebook)
Subjects: LCSH: Dolphins--Juvenile literature. | Porpoises--Juvenile literature.
Classification: LCC QL737.C432 S4286 2023 (print) | LCC QL737.C432 (ebook) | DDC 599.53--dc23/eng/20220104
LC record available at https://lccn.loc.gov/2021062909
LC ebook record available at https://lccn.loc.gov/2021062910

Text copyright © 2023 by Bellwether Media, Inc. BLASTOFF! READERS and associated logos are trademarks and/or registered trademarks of Bellwether Media, Inc.

Editor: Elizabeth Neuenfeldt   Designer: Laura Sowers

Printed in the United States of America, North Mankato, MN.

Table of Contents

Dolphins and Porpoises	4
Different Looks	8
Different Lives	16
Side by Side	20
Glossary	22
To Learn More	23
Index	24

Dolphins and Porpoises

Dolphins and porpoises are **mammals**. They look a lot alike!

dolphin

Both animals swim. They live in oceans and rivers. Do you know who is who?

porpoise

Different Looks

Dolphins are long and thin. Porpoises are shorter and wider.

Dolphins have long, **curved** top **fins**. Porpoises have shorter top fins. They look like triangles.

fin

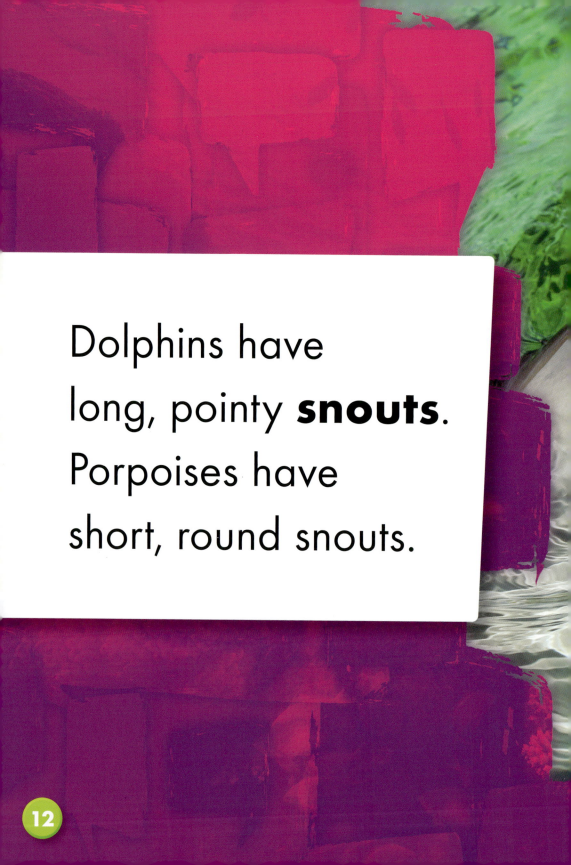

Dolphins have long, pointy **snouts**. Porpoises have short, round snouts.

snout

Porpoises have round teeth. Dolphins have pointy teeth.

Different Lives

Porpoises live alone or in small groups. Dolphins may live in big groups.

Dolphins **leap** out of the water. Porpoises usually do not. Who is this?

Side by Side

long, curved top fin

long, pointy snout

long, thin body

Dolphin Differences

can live in big groups

leap out of the water

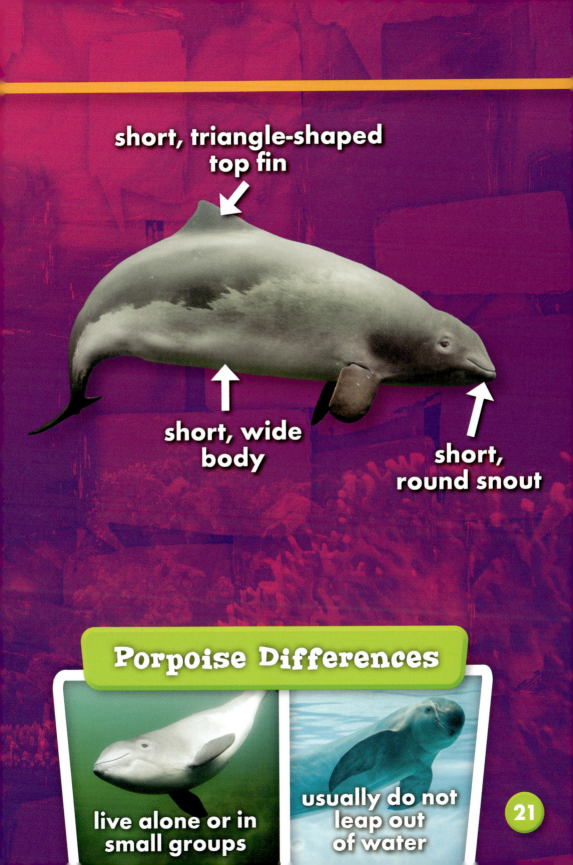

short, triangle-shaped top fin

short, wide body

short, round snout

Porpoise Differences

live alone or in small groups

usually do not leap out of water

Glossary

curved

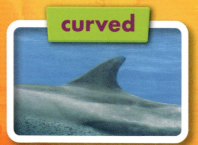

having a bend

mammals

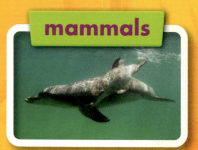

warm-blooded animals that have backbones and feed their young milk

fins

thin, flat parts that stick out from the bodies of some ocean animals

snouts

the noses and mouths of some animals

leap

to jump

To Learn More

AT THE LIBRARY

Amin, Anita Nahta. *Is It a Dolphin or a Porpoise?* North Mankato, Minn.: Pebble, 2022.

Leed, Percy. *Dolphins: A First Look.* Minneapolis, Minn.: Lerner Publications, 2023.

Pearson, Marie. *Dolphins and Porpoises.* Mankato, Minn.: The Child's World, 2020.

ON THE WEB

FACTSURFER

Factsurfer.com gives you a safe, fun way to find more information.

1. Go to www.factsurfer.com.

2. Enter "dolphin or porpoise" into the search box and click 🔍.

3. Select your book cover to see a list of related content.

Index

animals, 6
fins, 10, 11
groups, 16
leap, 18
live, 6, 16
mammals, 4
oceans, 6
rivers, 6
shape, 8
snouts, 12, 13
swim, 6

teeth, 14
water, 18

The images in this book are reproduced through the courtesy of: Andrea Izzotti, front cover (dolphin); Nature Picture Library/ Alamy, front cover (porpoise), pp. 10-11, 16-17; gilkop, pp. 4-5; C-images/ Alamy, pp. 6-7; megablaster, pp. 8-9; mauritius images GmbH/ Alamy, pp. 9, 21 (porpoise); Sabena Jane Blackbird/ Alamy, pp. 12-13; Gervasio S._Eureka_89, p. 13; Ian Scott, pp. 14-15; Jona Sanchez, p. 17; Tory Kallman, pp. 18-19; Potapov Alexander, p. 20 (dolphin); Lance Sagar, p. 20 (live in big groups); Chanonry, p. 20 (leap); Buiten-Beed/ Alamy, p. 21 (live alone); Vanhop, p. 21 (don't leap); COULANGES, p. 22 (curved); Gonzalo Jara, p. 22 (fins); Pascale Gueret, p. 22 (leap); Samantha Haebich, p. 22 (mammals); Arterra Picture Library/ Alamy, p. 22 (snouts).